That Kind of Happy

PHOENIX POETS

MAGGIE DIETZ

That Kind of Happy

THE UNIVERSITY OF CHICAGO PRESS

Chicago & London

MAGGIE DIETZ is the author of *Perennial Fall*, also published by the
University of Chicago Press, and coeditor of *Americans' Favorite Poems*,
Poems to Read, and *An Invitation to Poetry*. She teaches at the University
of Massachusetts Lowell.

The University of Chicago Press, Chicago 60637
The University of Chicago Press, Ltd., London
© 2016 by The University of Chicago
All rights reserved. Published 2016.
Printed in the United States of America

25 24 23 22 21 20 19 18 17 16   1 2 3 4 5

ISBN-13: 978-0-226-34939-8 (paper)
ISBN-13: 978-0-226-34942-8 (e-book)
DOI: 10.7208/chicago/9780226349428.001.0001

Library of Congress Cataloging-in-Publication Data

Dietz, Maggie, author.
    That kind of happy / Maggie Dietz.
        pages cm — (Phoenix poets series)
    ISBN 978-0-226-34939-8 (pbk. : alk. paper) —
ISBN 978-0-226-34942-8 (e-book)
    I. Title. II. Series: Phoenix poets.
    PS3604.I375T47 2016
    811'.6—dc23

                                    2015026770

♾ This paper meets the requirements of ANSI/NISO Z39.48-1992
(Permanence of Paper).

for RICHARD J. DIETZ

CONTENTS

ACKNOWLEDGMENTS

Grateful acknowledgment is made to the editors of the publications in which the following poems first appeared, some as earlier versions:

Agni: "November" and "Lullaby"
Cincinnati Review: "April Incantation"
Fifth Wednesday Journal: "When/Then"
Harvard Review: "Pluto"
Ibbetson Street: "Another Day, Another Dolor"
New South: "Hill Country," "Fiddle Ode," and "October Aubade"
Ploughshares: "Anywhere Elsewhere" and "Demolition Derby"
Poetry International: "Diagnosis Dream" and "One God"
Post Road: "Mediterranean" and "Galilee"
Provincetown Arts: "Still Falling"
Salamander: "December," "Killdeer," and "Two Shores"
Salmagundi: "Kempie," "Downtown," "Love Song," "Late Spring," and "Are We There Yet?"
Tar River Poetry: "Thin Ice" and "Takedown"
The Threepenny Review: "Zoloft"

"Pluto" was featured on *Verse Daily* and on MBTA Red Line trains in Boston through Mass Poetry's PoeTry program. "Anywhere Elsewhere" was reprinted in the Alhambra Poetry Calendar. "Slip" was written as a collaboration with the visual artist and sculptor Cat Chow for *Convergence: The Poetic Dialogue Project*, a traveling exhibition of works by twenty teams of visual artists and poets, curated by Beth Shadur and launched at the Ukrainian Institute of Modern Art in Chicago in February 2015.

Some of these poems were written with support from an individual artist fellowship from the New Hampshire State Council on the Arts.

Special thanks to the University of Massachusetts Lowell.

I owe a huge debt of gratitude to Robert Pinsky and Jill McDonough, and fathomless thanks to Todd Hearon, first best reader and fellow traveler.

ZOLOFT

Two weeks into the bottle of pills, I'd remember
exiting the one-hour lens grinder at Copley Square—
the same store that years later would be blown
black and blood-spattered by a backpack
bomb at the Marathon. But this was back when
terror happened elsewhere. I walked out
wearing the standard Boston graduate student
wire-rims, my first-ever glasses, and saw little people
in office tower windows working late under fluorescent
lights. File cabinets with drawer seams blossomed
wire bins, and little hands answered little black
telephones, rested receivers on bloused shoulders—
real as the tiny flushing toilets, the paneled wainscoting
and armed candelabras I gasped at as a child in
the miniatures room at the Art Institute in Chicago.

It was October and I could see the edges
of everything—where the branches had been a blur
of fire, now there were scalloped oak leaves, leathery
maple five-points plain as on the Canadian flag.
When the wind lifted the leaves the trees went pale,
then dark again, in waves. Exhaling manholes,
convenience store tiled with boxed cigarettes
and gum, the BPL's forbidding fixtures lit
to their razor tips and Trinity's windows holding
individual panes of glass between bent metal like

hosts in a monstrance. It was wonderful. It made me
horribly sad.

                              It was the same
years later with the pills. As I walked across
the field, the usual field, to the same river, I felt
a little burst of joy when the sun cleared a cloud.
It was fricking Christmas, and I was five years old!
I laughed out loud, picked up my pace: the sun
was shining on *me*, on the trees, on the whole
damn world. It was exhilarating. And sad,
that sham. Nothing had changed. Or
I had. But who wants to be that kind of happy?
The lenses, the doses. Nothing should be that easy.

HILL COUNTRY

At one with the febrile heat, the breathing acres,
We set out from the cinctured pasture.

Past the fencepost where we burst junk bottles
Into cullet with a borrowed gun, we followed

The broken cattle path through breaks in barbed wire,
Through hip-high switchgrass and snares of greenbrier

Into a cedar thicket so braided in places we had to double
Back or break through branches. We scrabbled

Up the back of a limestone cliff, our faces
Lit and muscles thrumming, until we surfaced

In the sky and could trace the green cleft of creek
Clear into the next county. We ignored the shrieks

Of buzzards gyring rot and, after our descent,
Stepped over a cottonmouth, curled like excrement

In a creek pool, crushing minnows with its face.
Hellbent on pleasure we fought through feral space

Until at last we lay in wildflowers, electrified
And spent, a network of nerve ray singeing the field,

Our skin imprinted with the spindly flowers
Of the skeleton plants swung over us like scythes.

ARE WE THERE YET?

On the drive from Des Moines, deer along the highway's
    gravel shoulder. Deer's eyes flaring
        from corridors of corn.

Lithe, narrow-faced silhouettes of deer
    beneath rare mosquito-swarmed streetlights,
        more numerous than the streetlights

floating above alfalfa, soybeans, hay,
    the grid of roads dividing fields from fields.
        Death is like the softest scarf settling

over your face. My grandfather knew this
    because he'd died a year before he died.
        He'd felt it, wasn't afraid. That night

the deer were spirits drifting, foraging, so many
    souls of the damned. Hundreds surfaced
        as you drove, and twice

I saw the handkerchief drifting down
    from heaven, felt it brush my eyes,
        my chin. A yearling first,

and, miles later, a sharp-racked buck, leapt
    onto the road in front of the car, the larger
        it seemed right over the ticking hood.

Death is silk, is cashmere. It wasn't how
      I wanted us to end. Didn't we
            make it to sunrise? I thought so,

I was certain. I remember the dew across the even stalks
      like sheets of muslin, the phosphorescent lake
            hung with mist.

KILLDEER

The bird limped through my dreams,
my days. I'd seen it
for two weeks, stitching steps
across the ball field, swift
as a jacket zipper.

It'd see me coming and rake
one wing across
the grass, hitch in its giddy-up,
coarse notes pitched
from its throat, a trick
to draw me away

from the naked nest—nothing
but a couple of pebbles, a few
strands of dry grass
tufting three ink-stippled
ivory eggs smooth
as dalmatian jasper.

How brutally stupid it must have
looked the morning the room-
sized rotary mower cleared
the field: the bird's
gimp instinct, rising cries—

unnoticed by the driver
and nothing to the blade.

DOWNTOWN

Hard not to notice the necklace
in the window, flashing in shadows
of passersby, draped on a stand
of flocked foam whose design
suggests clavicles, an attenuated
elegance even in the partial.
The pendant a threaded cymbal
or temple gong suspended from
strands of embroidery thread strung
at the base with carved, coral-painted
wooden beads then wound into twisted
ropes of glass—beads red and tiny as
tobiko—that meet in a loop and
coin clasp. Nothing I would wear:
nonetheless appealing, nonetheless
arresting in its almost-gaudy exoticism.
I'd like to meet who buys it. I'd like to
see in fifty years the granddaughter
with unusual taste inherit it, wear it with
jeans and a t-shirt and earrings she bought
for a song. I already miss her, that curious
girl from later, her bright eyeliner.
I've already gasped the day on the subway
the loop lost hold and the mercurial
beads went instantly everywhere, spraying
the seats like so many drops of blood.

SLIP

I. ORIGIN MYTH

Here is the cluttered warehouse, machines
    whirring in the airless heat.

New Delhi, let's say 1982. Here is the child
    seamstress: anonymous girl

we must give a name to, Indu, so we can
    envision her yawning as she lifts

two contoured panels from the pile beside her.
    The fabric cotton organdy

the color of milled chickpeas, color of some
    envisioned buyer's body, white

woman half a world away - - - Indu winds
    the bobbin to match the spool, hums

low so she can't be heard above the machines'
    shrill song, hums as if her song

could lift a string to spin the busted ceiling fan.
    She's good at her work, was told

by the twelve-year-old foreman her hands
    are nimble. Already risen

from floor to table, she used to snip loose threads
    from men's shirts in the circle

of hunched girls with curve-tip scissors. This
    is better - - - Now the feed dog chews

the fabric indifferently up and down across
    the throat plate as Indu depresses

the pedal, her fingers steering stitches. Let's say
    she's hungry, days since she's had

anything but roti. Let's say she has to go
    but holds her urine till it burns

because she fears the rats in the hall, the
    brimming toilet hole. Let's say

she smiles anyway (little girl) when it's time
    to affix the tulle, thinks

of a story she heard in school before
    her mother's sickness:

Princess Gulizar from Ivory City, who tried
    to poison the vizier's son

and repented. Such adventure when the royal
    elephants got loose! Such grandeur

when Gulizar left town with her prince and his
   magnificent retinue - - - Indu takes up

a tab, stitches *Made in India* into a seam, and then
   a larger label she can't read

though she admires its diving birds: *Hopeless
   Romantic* in faux Victorian script.

2. ADRIFT

Here it is hanging in
a Chicago thrift shop, years
after its department store
debut, still pristine, the v-
neck scalloped by ivory
waves and roses, the flounce
trim intact, in need of
fluffing up, donated by
its original owner, a
lipsticked housewife or
closeted cross-dresser,
some Carol or Thomas,
who'd wanted a little lift
from the tulle, to feel
dressed up undressing,
who'd wanted to be
wanted, admired,
loved. So much
for that.

One day
a young woman, blunt
bangs, smart tattoos,
will pull it from the jam
of wire hangers, admire its
clean lines, webbed hem,
both simple and fancy,
something ethereal in
its sheer weight, the way
on the hanger the sides
fan open as if occupied.
She'll wear it as a dress
to one of tomorrow's
parties, will love the way
its thin cotton moves
over her thin frame, and
other eyes will drink in
the liquefaction of her clothes
as she spins her bike
tires back to her place
at first light, staining
the slip with mud spatter
and guttered rain.

KEMPIE

When I was like you no one
spoke to me. For a while I'd see
you only while I slept: smoky reels
of silent family films, often
on your birthday. Not anymore.
You're cartwheeling past the window
now, brown shoes flickering like birds.
Scuff-kneed with square teeth
and a laugh like a rifle-shot—
too big for your britches, kid.
If you're so smart, what's taking you
so long? So the universe is huge,
plenty of people find their way.
There's a picture you drew on
the fridge, a blue walrus. There's
a story you wrote about a kangaroo.
Look, take any room. I'm sorry
I resisted giving up the study.
Let's put it behind us. Remember
when you didn't have the croup?
I stayed up all night making steam.
Remember when you didn't win
the spelling bee? We were so proud.
Dust and stars, the roads between
the moon and sun. The spokes
of light wheeling through the

room. Where are you living?
I keep missing you. Stubborn girl,
if you're waiting for some better
future it's too late. You've got a mother,
Kempie, and you've got a name.

DECEMBER

Nine days since we've seen the sun, the clouds
buried in clouds. Light falls in vellum strands
like ice from wires. The river's splintered pane

belies a warmer future. So we enter
another childless winter. Another month,
another season drifts into another year.

Who will want the mantel clock? Who will
phone on Tuesday afternoons? No body
to bury, no ghost to carry across our sleep.

Another morning's envelope will open.
The note enclosed will say no sun again.

AFTERNOON AT THE ER

Ordinary embarrassment downgrades
to humiliation when the physician's
assistant announces, as if delivering
a bona fide diagnosis: "You wanted
to fly." Oh, *you* want to fly, I think.
I erupted into a whimsical sprint on
the open beach in fourteen degrees
and bad shoes. There seems to be

no doctor, only helpers. A nurse with
an English accent jokes, "She's at that age
when you start to fall apart," not to me,
but to the technician in a purple smock
and ducky-printed turtleneck who wheels
me to the x-ray room that still smells
like her lunch.

                    "You pregnant?" she asks.
I'm not. My foot throbs—wrecked ball,
bloated big toe warping purple.

A *Woman's Day* later they tell me nothing
is broken. Nothing's broken, I repeat
to the husband there to take me home.

GALILEE

Much of what there was to see was dull:
mouse and ass and sparrow, snake in sand.

But gold in wool and temple, empire.
Wine-red pomegranates in the trees.

The roof over the sea cerulean calm days,
others as drab as fish gut or ash.

The sun an eye to some, to some a coin.
Mornings, hell in the heavens warning

sailors to heed the deep beneath them.
Evening come, the wild pale horses

of the waves delivered fishers to fish,
made widows of small-fisted women,

husbands of brothers. Sabbaths the wind
wouldn't rest, infants tested their lungs.

Late sacrifices blazed on an altar where
a poor man prayed, then stole the bread.

Beggars, clothed in nerves, bellowed.
A girl crouched at an open window.

Above the fuss of lovers' grunts and
lepers' bells, the white rustling of wings.

LATE SPRING

In a bath with baking soda the boy pondered
the vanished bird: spindly wings netted with veins,
tufts of fuzz at the wattled throat, the skin there
pink and feathered as an old man's neck
or hand. Black eyes visible through skeins
of lids. The soft pink belly like a clam.

Later he'd dream of swimming in air without
a float or wings, of a raw chicken in a pot
of wine and herbs, and the bald neighbor
who spoke by holding a box to his throat.

It had dropped from the elm to the driveway.
The boy had watched it whine and rasp,
then fetched a flour sack and his doctor's kit.

The scalding water pinked his skin, pruned
his finger bulbs so that he couldn't see the whorls.
His mother dipped a toothbrush in acetone,
scrubbed beneath the child's transparent nails.

She put the boy to bed, the bandaged bird,
expired, between the fence and garden shed,
the toy stethoscope in a bowl of bleach—
clean of its work, its good intentions.

All night, the elm swam in its net of stars.
Disease would take it and the neighbor
but not that summer, not that night.

The boy swam circles around the old man's
metal lawn chair. The chicken danced
in its savory bath and the old man sang like
a gramophone or robot *so remember this, life is no abyss,*
somewhere there's a bluebird of happiness as green crabapples
plunked from the branches onto macadam.

DELIVERY

I. WAKING

First the low drone of
uilleann pipes, the river
of the spine just barely
quivering: the froth
on a half-drunk pint
of Guinness shifting
as the bellows breathes.

2. WAITING

A pressure sprouting
in the back—the joke
I told about having
eaten a pumpkin seed
to astonish the moon-
faced toddler gawping
at my beach ball belly
in the grocery line.

3. PITOCIN

What the   hell is this
no one said   chaos I
can't find the   cerulean
beach, the sun-   rayed
trail through   rain-cooled
woods can't   find your
face the   soft flamenco
music   hurts I
hate   it you
turn   off
it   now

4. LIDOCAINE

Flying bullets, bats,
then, finally, birds.
Swallows sky-diving
for mosquitos above
the quiet reservoir
at dusk. Iridescent
synchronicity, twisting
together as if on
strings. You must
listen hard to hear
the soft applause of
(closed in unison)
a thousand wings.

5. PARTURITION

Hosannas in the skull
halls: I see as if from
above a body brought
to its knees, every one
of its live cells singing

Hosanna for "we praise
you" and "please save
us" as being trains its
way into the lighted
room, the ravaged world.

LOVE SONG

The ancients would lift
    a clay spout to your lips—
    water and honey and wine.

I give you milk, softened
    with wine, and swear

you'll never hunger, never
    thirst while I'm alive.

What suffering I can't preclude
    I'll soothe with singing:

My future, for you

not the greenness of a leaf
    but of the leaves on all
    the April branches.

Fire, I give you fuel. I sweat
    and chop the wood.

I tender forever in you
    who begin where I end as if

your body is
    my body, your elegance
    my elegance.

Sustenance, emptiness
    is lack of you, yearning is

the road to where you are.

You are the road, the where,
    the song, the hunger. Child,

I give you sleep, I sing
                    you there.

DIAGNOSIS DREAM

We sit together at the table of sleep:
brown-eyed maple set with fine bone

china, heavy silver. A horse snuffs
in the corner. The eyes in the wood

grain blink, watch us as we wait
to eat the untold dishes steaming

in lidded tureens. The horse neighs.
There's news, you say. You say

the news.
          Now

the table's a bridge and you are on
the other side. My legs can't climb

up without failing. Without you
I cannot get to you. You're riding

the dining horse, already tiny
on the horizon. You don't see me

trying. When I cry out the sky
eats your name. The wind

thickens. Water wells up under
the bridge. The glazed tureens float

by me. One by one, I lift the lids:
empty, empty, empty, empty.

ONE GOD

God built our house. God
is a builder of things. Is God
a lady? God is a mommy.

We can't hear God. We can
yell *God, where are you?*
God is far away. God can't

hear us. God is a man
old lady little boy. God's not
a person! God is a doctor.

Can God make my wart
fall off? Bob fall off his bike,
God help him. God fall

off his car and Bob be nice
to him. God has a dinosaur
car. God's a her. God lives

in our tummy. God a baby.
God makes Papa not be
sick. God's a bird, I think.

OCTOBER AUBADE

If I slept too long, forgive me.

A north wind quickened the window frames
so the room pitched like a moving train

and the pillow's whiff of hickory
and shaving soap conjured your body

beside me. So I slept in the berth
as the train chuffed on, unburdened

by waking's cold water, ignorant
of pain, estrangement, hunger and

the crucial fuel the boiler burned
to keep the minutes' pistons churning

while I slept. Forgive me.

NOVEMBER

Show's over, folks. And didn't October do
A bang-up job? Crisp breezes, full-throated cries
Of migrating geese, low-floating coral moon.

Nothing left but fool's gold in the trees.
Did I love it enough, the full-throttle foliage,
While it lasted? Was I dazzled? The bees

Have up and quit their last-ditch flights of forage
And gone to shiver in their winter clusters.
Field mice hit the barns, big squirrels gorge

On busted chestnuts. A sky like hardened plaster
Hovers. The pasty river, its next of kin,
Coughs up reed grass fat as feather dusters.

Even the swarms of kids have given in
To winter's big excuse, boxed-in allure:
TVs ricochet light behind pulled curtains.

The days throw up a closed sign around four.
The hapless customer who'd wanted something
Arrives to find lights out, a bolted door.

PLUTO

Don't feel small. We all have
been demoted. Go on being

moon or rock or orb, buoyant
and distant, smallest craft ball

at Vanevenhoven's Hardware
spray-painted purple or day-glow

orange for a child's elliptical vision
of fish line, cardboard and foam.

No spacecraft has touched you,
no flesh met the luster of your

heavenly body. Little cold one, blow
your horn. No matter what you are

planet, and something other than
planet, ancient but not "classical,"

the controversy over what to call you
light-hours from your ears. On Earth

we tend to nurture the diminutive,
root for the diminished. None

of your neighbors knows your name.
Nothing has changed. If Charon's

not your moon, who cares? She
remains unmoved, your companion.

DEMOLITION DERBY

Amped-up grid lights growl stars
onto the hay-baled dirt ring,

onto blistered chrome and rust-lace,
car shells taped and painted over

to resemble shapes of cars. We're
bleachered, gum-shoed, bleached

by glare, sloshing beer and sponging
powdered sugar from our shirt-

fronts. Rumbles in the air,
our guts, the gears chunking

and purring, the stands gnashing,
owling Os. At the flag, the cornered

cars spring almost sprightly
for an instant, then hunch-buckle

into each other, crumple in smoke.
I am in love. With Todd and Jill

and Bob I bash myself through
minutes booing besters, leaning

into lurchers seeking comebacks.
Rev-engined mish-mash, mosh

pit of metal, brand-emblazoned
junk-car smash-'em-up. Trash

rodeo, trough pigs brawling over
scraps and swill. O plastic tumblers

of shwag-brew in Topsfield under an
October moon. O wrestling angels:

hum and bash your hymn of
destruction, breach and belch your

tailpipe spit and prayer. We're happy
here where nothing doesn't hurt.

ANOTHER DAY, ANOTHER DOLOR

That one morning as you straightened
your Shakespeare theme-tie before heading off
to teach Hamlet, you sighed and said in your
whack Spanish "El otro día, el otro dinero!"
And I sighed bigger and said "Yes—
the other day, the other money."

Or the time I was trying not to spill wine on a pile
of papers, writing tiny hieroglyphs
in too-big margins, and you
kept coming in so finally mean-voiced
I said "Let me work!" and you said,
"I am the grass" then (half-beat)
over your shoulder: "Smoke me."

But that wasn't as good as the day my parents
were trying to remember the first name
of some former mayor of Green Bay
on the same day a baby bunny got stuck
in their garage and after dinner my mom
was half-dozing when my dad came in and said
"The bunny is out. And his name is Paul."
And my mom said "How do you know
his name is Paul?" And realizing she meant
the bunny he said "Because I checked
his little wallet and found his little ID!"

Then there was that time not two years
later in a fluorescent hospital room when
he was in and out of morphine sleep
and we'd all four kids come from our lives
for his dying and Mom was there of course
and Dad woke up from, we imagined, an
ancestral dream and seemed surprised
to see us though we'd been there bedside
for days and he cleared his throat—
we angled in to hear if he'd say something
wise—and he did he said "I guess
you're wondering why I called this meeting."

STILL FALLING

Crisp and brittle the leaves, the branches,
Broken and blanched the bones, the ashes.
Ashes coat the ghost-gray branches.

Tusks of steel, the busted girders,
Skulls of rooms; the sun's ghost lingers
Over skewed pipes and crusts of windows

Scattered among the shattered people.
Later the moon, a flake of opal,
Oversees the writhing rubble:

Fingers of smoke sift and thicken.
Ashen figures swarm the smitten
Grave. They light and listen—

Even the living are ghosts, are history.
All bewilderment, no mystery.
Fuel smolders in the blistering

Smear of heat, the voices calling.
Somehow it's the dark unveiling
The ruin of this still fresh, still falling.

FIDDLE ODE

Fidget-rig there's whiskey in you—
get the bow to smoking. Whittle our
jollies into a jig, a ramble through
brambles of luck and blunder so
rollicking blood thunders into our
cheeks, time into our feet. Fly and dive
on horsehair wings: clip the crotchet to
bow a triple note. Cut the pitch and flick
and stutter your bird-call question: more
vigor than rigor or rigor than vigor?

Then land, little bird, on the low branch
of a weeping birch. Now, creature,
keen. Tune the strings to Skibbereen.
Ply ancestral aching through the wires
of time. Peel open bygone grief and loose
old loneliness. Ask *why* and answer
yes. Sing us to raw waters wrought
with loss, to harder shores, the dregs
of a drained glass.

THIN ICE

The dog won't cross the field.
He can remember pain, last
winter's snow-crazed footpads.

The frozen river's like a place
in me I mustn't go, so I cross
the field myself in the fog
of my own breath.

Bittersweet and winterberry
edge the gossamer ice, bright
metal hammered fine as the
ghost of a ghost of the moon.

But it's not beauty I'm after.
Near the footbridge a sign
shows a stick man thrashing
in the black arms of an asterisk.

You can tell he's getting tired.
He's mouthing the DANGER
I came to remember.

TERMS OF THE DISEASE

The lung the lining the
lymph nodes the liver,
bones in the hip and
spine. Oat cell small
cell extensive PET-scan
carcinoma recurring
terminal.

Metastatic cisplatin
prognosis etoposide
prophylactic (elective)
cranial irradiation.

Nadir neuropathy
(peripheral) complete
response (*we don't say
remission*). Months or
weeks or—

Oral topotecan doses,
multiple masses: the
lung the lining the
lymph nodes the liver
the spine the brain
morphine

LULLABY

After Lyle Lovett

If I had a gingko tree
I'd climb it in the evening.

If I had a marmoset
He'd climb the tree with me.

If we saw a falling star
I'd wish I had a rocket.

If I had a rocket
I'd drag the star back home.

If I went to space
I'd pick up a satellite.

If I had my own moon
I wouldn't be so sad.

If I weren't so sad
I wouldn't need a companion.

If I sold my marmoset
I'd have a lot of cash.

If I had some money
I'd buy an Eldorado.

49

(Silver, 1959,
With fins like raptor wings.)

I'd shine that Eldorado
and drive it to my father's.

If I had a father
I'd take him for a ride.

TAKEDOWN

Since you died
I've been pinned

down. I'm weak,
can't outmaneuver

grief, can't grapple
to ungrip its hold

even when it's hard
to breathe or when

I cramp for want
of water. I fail

even at surrender:
When I say uncle

it comes out *father*.

APRIL INCANTATION

O wrathful rain roll down
and down. Outwit the drains,

unground us. Wind and thunder,
steer the torrent's train and throw

us under. Upriver, water, rage
and rack the dam to shatter. Blast

the happy poppies. Let petal-
blood trouble the flooded field.

Crack new bourns and boundaries
into parceled plots. Wreck even

the season that reared you: lick
the lilacs into sobbing heaps.

Flounce the furrows and swallow
the seeds. Gut the leaf-

rucked gutters. Wrestle reed
beds into rags. Wrench up head-

stones, grub the graves and spit
the picked bones in the ocean.

Show us nothing's sacred,
nothing safe. Fair enough. I fed

this flood. I'll take my place
among the fallen sodden.

WHEN/THEN

When in the morning night's still on me,
thick in the limbs and in the coffee,
bleak in my mouth, silt in the teeth,
breaking the back of the clock to hold me;

and the blanks of my eyes cool stars,
and the stars in my gut gone out
except where they shoot or burst—
the moon of your being blue, remote;

when the window's through and through
it the broken-winged crow
coughs its small hell into all
we are; then I drag down the hall

to the room where the baby moans
till I blur over her, a working sun.

TWO SHORES

My little boat can
only go so far.
The coiled rope
unwinds from
the dock to just
about midway
across the lake—
the point where
the trees on the other
shore unblur—
before the horn
cleat catches.

The tether is
a voice, two
voices, a need
that is a weight,
a rope or hook.

Back on shore
the voices grow
toes and elbows,
scramble to be
held, kissed, to lift
wet faces to my
mouth. To hold

them is to hurt
with joy. Bodies
still small enough
I can gather both in
my butterflied skirt.

But whose were
the cries from the
other shore my
muscles burned
for as I rowed?

MEDITERRANEAN

All around us ochre cliffs
fortify the fading sky.
A market square hums
its wares of almond, saffron
and new wine. These, Picasso's
cobbled streets, his angles
and orange trees. Everything
whole, all the wholes long ago
broken. Bread, the bombed
out bridge of Pont du Loup.
Bright villages built into the hills.
I'd like to say the words flown
down the road, the birds I can't
pronounce, to you. Here under
an unfamiliar sun, taste with me
the sounds I cannot say. Help
lift the hillside to my mouth.

ANYWHERE ELSEWHERE

How anybody makes it in this country
I don't know. Any way you turn
there is an edge, and everyone
cocks a wind-burned hand over
the brow to look out under it.
The water flings petticoats of foam
against wolf-headed rocks, and
multicolored boats moored
among others to the weathered
pier bob dumb as soldiers.
We live on what's beneath us.
Dark snake-like birds curl into
the water, rise like rose blooms
floated in bowls. And every day
the riven, mended nets go trolling.
A far cry from my unforgotten fields.
How is it then the boat lamps
and the buoy bells dislocate me?—
aching not for home, for something
I can't name. As if I could be half-
another, as if I've lived someplace
I never will. Winter brought greenish
bergs to the harbor, floes composed
of further waters. And the strange
white crows here rode them.
A mustached woman poured

scalding coffee on the feet of one
to free it from the scalloped ice
night layered on the sand.
It screamed as my lost brother
does in dreams, with a creature's
anguished hatred. Next morning,
it lay in the wheat-colored grass,
half-eaten by dogs. Here, shells
resembling army helmets wash
ashore, and cataracted eyes of horses.
The town creaks, the seaward shingles
of the dry-faced widows' houses
loosen like teeth. A squall will snap
a mast in half clean as a bone.
Are we not shipwrecked?
The gravid sea holds nothing
for us—but how we squint out
over it, waiting for another sun,
for someone else's blessèd hour.

NOTES

p. 14: "Slip," part 2 ("Adrift"). The line "the liquefaction of her clothes" comes from Robert Herrick's lyric "Upon Julia's Clothes."

p. 15: "Kempie." The name Kempie comes from a traditional American folk song titled "Mole in the Ground." Different versions of the song include variations on the name: Kimpy, Tewkie, Gimpie, Tempe, Kippy, Kimby, Tippy, etc.

p. 37: "Pluto." In 2006, the International Astronomical Union created an official definition for the term "planet." Pluto did not meet all three of the definition's criteria and was reclassified by the Union as a "dwarf planet," inciting debate among scientists as well as significant public uproar.

p. 41: "Another Day, Another Dolor." The second stanza makes reference to Carl Sandburg's widely anthologized poem "Grass," which ends with the lines: "I am the grass. / Let me work."